MW00790586

DIRT CHEAP REAL ESTATE

THE ULTIMATE 5 STEP SYSTEM FOR A BROKE BEGINNER TO GET INSANE ROI BY FLIPPING AND INVESTING IN VACANT LAND BUILD YOUR PASSIVE INCOME WITH NO MONEY DOWN

BEAUX BLAST

WWW.BEAUXBLAST.COM

PUBLISHED BY LUCK AND PROSPERITY PUBLISHING HOUSE

CONTENTS

ACKNOWLEDGEMENTS

To everyone I passed on my journey - I couldn't have done it without you.

I especially want to thank my family. You are the reason I started investing and your support is the reason I succeeded. Without you, I would not have started investing and I could not have written this book.

To the reader, I hope I help you as others have helped me. I wrote this book because I am tired of seeing people give up. This is the age of information, where you can find anything you need online! And yet, so many people are getting scammed... I don't want that to be you. Anyone who reads this book will be armed with the knowledge they need to get started, pick the right mentors, and find success. Thank you for giving me a chance to change your life.

LAND INVESTING CHECKLIST BUNDLE

(SUPERCHARGE YOUR BUSINESS!)

THIS COMPANION BUNDLE INCLUDES:

- A Quickstart checklist for finding your perfect investment area
- The Due Diligence Checklist: NEVER miss a due diligence step again
- A BONUS FLOWCHART: Busting through common seller objections

The last thing we want is for you to start investing in unprofitable land and give up. Download this bundle to STOP that from happening.

To receive your Land Investing Checklist Bundle, visit the link:

LAND.BEAUXBLAST.COM

THREE REASONS WHY LAND INVESTING IS THE BEST WAY TO GET STARTED AS A BEGINNER

Whether you're trying to build passive income, quit your 9 to 5, or amass wealth, investing in land is an excellent choice. Land investing is lower risk, has a lower barrier to entry, and has been known to give over 100% returns in a matter of months.

When I first started investing, I followed my guru's advice and attended all of my local Real Estate Investing club's meetings. There are 4 clubs in my city: three of these clubs focused on residential investing and one focused on commercial. There were easily 50 investors in each of the residential investing clubs and over 200 in the commercial investing club! Over 350 people in my city were trying to invest in commercial or residential real estate. Now, my city is pretty big, but it certainly isn't big enough to handle that much competition.

Did some of those investors find success? Sure, but many didn't. How are you supposed to find deals when everyone else is using the exact same technique and working just as hard as you? Surprisingly, I did manage to find a few deals... but unsurprisingly, all of them ended in a bidding war. Bidding wars had 2 outcomes: either the deal would go to the more experienced investor or a new investor would buy it for way too much. Fortunately for me, I never could get a deal, so at least I didn't end up wasting any money.

To drive my point home, I'll tell you about one of the loveliest couples I met. They had started investing back in 2008, right after the market crashed, and were well established by the time I started investing in 2016. They had a huge network of lenders, a great online presence and a wonderful rapport with several of the local realtors. These couples bought around 20 properties per year, each one was completely unlivable and cost about 500k. They'd usually end up bulldozing the house (if you could call it that) and spending about 400k building a new, trendy one. After 9 months of bulldozing, then could usually sell them for a cool mil. How could I, a new investor with a couple thousand bucks, compete with a business like that?

As you know, the first rule of business is to create value and the second rule of business is to be different than your competitors. So, I did what any reasonable person would do and started looking at how I could create a business that was different from everyone else but still produced value.

And that's what led me to land investing.

Remember those REI club meetings I told you about? Out of those 350+ investors, how many do you think invested in land? Three. And they were making bank. I wouldn't have ever considered investing in land if I hadn't chanced upon them. After all, all the popular TV shows had taught me that investing in buildings was the way to go. Who would ever think you could make any money buying and selling empty lots?

So What is Land Investing?

Land investing is buying land that people don't want at a discount and selling it to people who do for almost full price.

Yep, that's it.

Why is Investing In Land So Much Better Than Other Investments or Businesses?

1. Land Investing is Lower Risk

Compared to other forms of Real Estate Investing, land investing is a much lower risk. For starters, you don't have to deal with the three T's of real estate. Tenants, termites, and toilets. Buildings come with a lot of problems that the average joe just doesn't want to deal with. Sure, if you're new to investing it probably sounds easy... but you've never been woken up at 3AM because a toilet overflowed. You've also never been told your investment was going to cost an extra 10k because of some unknown electrical issues you only managed to find after you closed. Ouch.

The next problem is the price. If you've ever seen a show on HGTV, you know that flipping a house is extremely costly. Land, on the other hand, is very cheap in comparison.

Sure, houses are expensive... but you get your money's worth in the end!

Unfortunately, while it looks really profitable on TV, they usually don't show you all the expenses that come with buying and selling a house - like paying the realtor, the closing fees, and the furnishing fees. To add insult to injury, inexperienced investors are much more likely to buy a property that has major hidden damage. So not only do new investors fail to figure in some costs on the backend, they might also miss costs on the front end. A bad roof and a miscalculation on closing fees can kill a deal. And I'm not even going into the issues I've seen with permits not being approved for months or even years on end, or the expensive holding costs that come with flipping a house.

Don't get me wrong, flipping can be extremely profitable if you know what you're doing... but it's 10x harder than land. There are far fewer things that can go wrong with land investing, so there is much less risk. What's more, I will eliminate 95% of that risk later on in chapter 3, when I explain due diligence.

Maybe you are still a skeptic - like the investors at my REI club - and believe that land is only valuable if you improve it. I don't blame you for feeling this way, but it isn't true. There are lots of people who want to buy raw land. For many people, owning a plot of land outside city limits is a dream they've had since childhood. Sure, you'll also sell to farmers, hunters, and co-ops, but many Americans dream of a little piece of this country they can call their own.

2. Lower Startup Cost

Investing in land has a lower startup cost when compared to other real estate. Investing in single-family homes(SFH) can cost tens of thousands of dollars... and that's just the down payment. Commercial investing will run you hundreds of thousands. That may not be a problem if you're starting with a lot of capital or have a network interested in investing with you... But if you don't have either of those things, then it is significantly harder to start. With land investing, you can find properties for as low as 500 bucks and easily double your money with a quick flip.

3. No Employees Needed

Any form of investing is a business. The good news about land investing is you don't need to pay any employees when you first start. It's true, as your business grows, you will hire some extra hands or outsource some tasks. But, in the beginning, it is 100% expected and reasonable to be the sole employee in your business. That means you have no employee overhead... So, all the profit goes straight to you.

1

HOW TO NOT WASTE YOUR MONEY

I used to check my bank account every day. It was the only thing I could do to force myself to continue grinding. Sometimes, my bank account was high, and other times it was low. Either way, I'd sigh, put my phone back in my pocket, and get back to work.

Then, I heard about investing. *Wow! You mean I can make money in my sleep?* The answer from the internet seemed to be a resounding YES! So, I started looking into every kind of investing known to man. I liked real estate because I could leverage my money...which was good because I didn't have a lot of money...

So, I started learning everything I could about real

estate. I had been an avid HGTV watcher, but I hadn't actually thought of flipping a house myself until I started thinking about my future. I soon learned that HGTV only showed half the story. I binged all of Biggerpockets podcasts, read every book, and watched every youtuber. Eventually, I paid for a formal "coach". I ponied up my money and was ready to work...

Funny how their best advice was to pay more money so I could join the "in-club" - a network of real estate investors who had insider information and would only do deals with other club members. You could find deals without joining, but it was like a mom and pop store trying to outsell Walmart - I simply didn't have enough money or time. After six months of hard work, I only had about $2000 to my name. Most of the successful investors in my town were spending that much per month on mailers alone! How could I compete with that? I had no money, and I only had so much time.

At the end of the 6 months, I started reevaluating my choices. I knew real estate was the way I wanted to grow my wealth... but I also knew that flipping was not the best option for me at the time.

- I needed something cost-effective.
- I needed a way to leverage my money.
- I needed an unsaturated market.
- I needed low risk

I'm hoping this book will help you skip the first six months of failure and get right to success. I don't want to promise you that I'm a master at land investing - but I do want to share what I've learned.

If you're starting out broke, you're probably very concerned about the startup costs of land investing. Hell, you're probably concerned even if you do have money. So, I'm going to break down all the costs. The costs range from less than a hundred bucks a month to thousands depending on how much you have to market and which marketing strategy you choose. But, the great thing about investing in land is that you don't need to stick to your county - you can invest anywhere because everything you need to do can be done online or hired out.

Investing online opens up the possibility of purchasing land that is dirt cheap because you aren't limited by location. If you find that an area is too competitive, you can easily find a new, untapped market! Unlike residential and commercial investing, land investing has not become mainstream yet, so there are hundreds of thousands of counties full of untapped potential.

Now that you know you can find a deal, let's look at the costs. I've broken it down into three sections.

Section 1: The Absolute Necessities and How To Get Them For Free. These are what I consider the necessary costs associated with investing in land. You will need at least these tools to get started.

Section 2: Costs that will Make Investing Easier but are not Necessary. These expenses will help your business become more efficient but are not necessary. If you are broke, you can get away with not spending any money here. However, when your business grows, you will naturally begin to use these tools.

Section 3: Unnecessary Startup Costs. I consider these expenses to be unnecessary to start investing. You will probably need them later on, but you do not need them the day you start. I advise you to stay away from these items because trying to do them will take up your time and slow you down.

If you have invested in Real Estate before or don't want to hear the reason behind each of the different expenses associated with investing in land, feel free to skip to the end of this chapter to see a tl;dr table.

I want to be upfront with you here - some of the services I recommend are through an affiliate link. This shouldn't deter you from using my link (after all, some of them come with a discount) because most of these service's competitors also have affiliate programs, so there is no reason to promote a service I don't believe in. With that out of the way, let's get into it!

SECTION 1: THE ABSOLUTE NECESSITIES AND HOW TO GET THEM FOR FREE

Education

You've already covered this first expense. For the price of this book, you get a wealth of knowledge on land investing. I am not saying you never need to purchase another book, explore a course or get a more expensive education... However, this book should get you 80% of the way there. Hell, if you follow the instructions in this book, you'll start investing in the next chapter.

There is a bit of a disclaimer. Since this book is for the entire continental US, there are a few things that

I simply cannot teach you because they are different for each state. Luckily, I will tell you how to find most of this information for free online. You will more than likely be investing in several states at one time, so you should be familiar with how to find this information online anyway.

If you do choose to purchase a course, this book gives you all the information you need to select one that will not scam you. I will make the bold assumption that you do not want to spend or do not have $20,000 for a guru that will attempt to teach you how to invest in land. I have had experience with these gurus, and while some people do find them very helpful, they are usually unnecessary. Trust me, they all teach the same stuff that I'm gonna share with you.

I know there are a few things a book can't do that a guru might. For example, I can't check up on you to make sure that you are taking action and I can't really answer your questions. To solve these deficiencies, I have included easy action items in each chapter, and I'm going to show you a few places where you can ask all of your questions for free.

Facebook

There are tons of open groups on Facebook about Land Investing. All you have to do is log on to Facebook and search for "Land Investing" in the top left corner. When investing, you will come across unique situations and wonder what to do. Normally, that's where a coach would come in, but sometimes they don't even know what to do...

However, if you join a free Facebook group, you have hundreds of free coaches. At least one person will have been in your situation before. Make sure you join as many of the groups as possible and ask all the questions that you can. Why not? It's free!

Well, why did I buy this book then?.

Good question! Because you need to know where to start. That's where this book comes in. It's 100% true, you could learn all this information for free by looking through all the forums for a few months (after all, that's kind of what I did!), but it's much more time effective to buy a book for a couple bucks and spend a few hours reading it. I know I'm going out on a limb here, but the price of this book is probably worth the time you would have otherwise spent learning the same information from several disjointed places on the web.

Youtube

After you've completed this book, you'll likely want to see some case studies or need some encouragement. Simply search for "Land Investing". You will find lots of great youtubers who are experts and are giving away their knowledge for free. Many of them even have Facebook groups that you can join.

Meetup

Meetup is a free app where you can find and join local groups. You should use this app to join as many REI groups as you possibly can! Why? Because other investors will be there. Go to every nearby meeting this month and meet as many investors as you can. Tell them you're interested in investing in land. If they are also interested in land deals, make sure you get their contact information! You do not need to have business cards, but you will need some paper to write down names and numbers. This is especially important if you are trying to start at $0. Many of these investors will be willing to pay you a finders fee or partner with you if you find a good deal. And, bonus - they will tell you if the deal you are considering is good or not *for free.* Why? Because if they don't want a stake in it, it's not a good deal.

Unfortunately, joining these groups could cost you up to $20/month. Usually your first session is free so don't be afraid. The networking is worth it.

However, If you are literally starting with 0$, stick to the Facebook groups and posting your questions in the meetup message board.

A word of caution - there are many ways to make money investing in Real Estate. Do not get seduced into doing menial tasks for these investors. Be focused on bringing them deals, asking their opinion, and partnering. After the first month or so, limit the amount of time you spend in these groups to 1 or 2 meetings per month. Most of them won't be land specific, so they won't be as useful. The only reason you need to go is to network.

Gurus

I hesitate to write about this, but I wanted to throw it in here for the sake of completeness. Gurus are great at selling you their course - but the best advice I got from my guru was to go to my local REI club and join Facebook groups to meet other investors. Other than that, I don't think he was very useful. I didn't learn anything from that coach that I didn't know before or didn't find out for free immediately.

I know that some of you are not self-starters and will ignore the action items in this book. If you are one of those people, I would suggest you passively invest in the stock market because investing in Real Estate is very time consuming in the beginning and takes a lot of determination. Some gurus will tell you that you should join their team because it's what you need to do to force yourself to work... but don't fall into this trap if you know it's not true.

After you read this book, you'll have a really solid foundation in land investing. You will be able to ask pointed questions and find a coach that will actually help you succeed instead of a guru who will just take your money. That being said, you should always ask around on Facebook or BiggerPockets before you pay for a course. There's nothing better than a recommendation from several people.

Low costs: $0

High Costs: $5000+

Lists

Lists are a crucial part of investing in any kind of real estate. Your REI club will probably focus on single-family homes, so you might hear a lot about canvassing neighborhoods. Canvassing is when you drive to a neighborhood and knock on every door. If someone answers, you ask that person if they know anyone who wants to sell their house. This will usually net one lead every nine hours. Typically, one out of three will be a good investment. That is what we call a horrible ROI. I don't know about you, but that sounds more like an awful job than investing to me.

Fortunately, land investing doesn't lend itself to canvassing because the owners don't live on their vacant or raw land. So, what do you do instead? Lists.

What are lists?

They are spreadsheets of people who are likely to sell their land.

Why are lists so great?

Lists will help you find motivated sellers. Not everyone on these lists will be a motivated land seller, but it is much more likely. These lists narrow down the amount of people you need to market to which means you will be wasting less of your time (and money!) trying to find good investments.

Where do I get these lists?

You can get them in a variety of ways. Some people will tell you to go to the county clerk's office and ask them if you can have a copy of the various lists that we will talk about in chapter 2. I would advise you to try using an online listing service first. The only advantage of a county list is freshness(if it's fresher, it has more up to date information).

While freshness is something we care about, I strongly recommend against going to the county clerk's office when you start investing because it is tough to communicate with the clerks. They do not all speak the same language as you... and I don't mean they don't speak English. Also, you will probably invest in an area far from where you live, so you will have to pay an assistant to grab the list for you. These lists can cost anywhere from $50 to $200 depending on what the clerks charge. That's a huge expense when you're just getting started!

What method do you recommend?

I recommend that you use a combination of free and cheap options online. I will show you how to get all of the lists you need online for either free or very discounted. Many investors exclusively use online lists and never have to deal with the county at all.

Low costs: $0/month

High Cost: $300/month

Finding Investments

The cheapest way to find properties is to keep an eye out on websites like Facebook Marketplace and Craigslist. I will give you more websites as well as instructions later on. Keep in mind that the free way is slow. It might take you a few months to find a great deal instead of a few weeks.

If you do have some money in your budget for marketing and would like to accelerate the process of finding a good investment, you can pay for some marketing. Finding good investments is the crux of your business, so it should be where you are devoting most of your time and money. I'll show you exactly what to do in chapter 2.

Low costs: $0/month

High costs: $2000/month

Property Acquisition

Ah yes, PURCHASING an investment. Surprisingly, you can do this for as little as $0. However, I recommend you have at least $1000 for this particular expense. Why $1000? Because the type of land we will be looking for will be deeply discounted. And if you happen upon land that isn't at a price you can afford, there are strategies you can use to purchase it for very little money down, which I will explain in detail later in chapter 4.

Low costs: $0

High costs: $1000

Holding Costs

New investors sometimes forget that there may be holding costs associated with some investments. If you follow the steps in this book, you will more than likely pay minimum holding costs, but for the sake of posterity, your holding costs will generally be the price of your loan (If you have one), the price of the HOA (If there is one), and the price of taxes (Only due at the end of the year). Normally, taxes are 1-4% of the land's appraised value. I would say you could probably get by with 0$ for this section.

Low costs: $0

High costs: $1000+

Selling costs

We will go over this in detail in chapter 5. Luckily, you'll be able to cover the selling costs from your profit, so you will likely have money by the time you need to pay for this expense. If you don't mind paperwork and learning about the legal process, your selling cost could be as low as $200, depending on the price of your land and the notary. However, I recommend you use a title company - it is worth the peace of mind.

When you do a deal, you generally make several thousand dollars, so it shouldn't be a problem. Title companies will run you maybe $500. If you do a double close, this $500 will include both the closing costs associated with selling and buying the property. More on that later.

The most expensive way to close a deal is to use a realtor. As investors, we want to be friends with realtors, but we don't want to use them to buy and sell. I will talk more about this in chapter 5, but if you're using a realtor, plan to allocate 10% of the purchase or sales price.

Low Costs: $200

High Costs: $1000+

Contract Templates

These are the legal documents used to purchase or sell property. If you have $40 and would like something official, you can use legal websites like Rocket-Lawyer.com. This website has every type of contract you could imagine, drafted by lawyers for your use. One document is $39.99, but if you join their subscription service for $39.99 per month, you get unlimited contracts and legal advice.

If you want to take a chance, you can get your contracts from Facebook groups and other Land investors that are willing to share them with you.

Low Costs: $0

High Costs: $39.99/month

Section 2: Costs that will Make Investing Easier but are not Necessary

Mailbox

We will talk about several ways to find motivated sellers in chapter 2, but a few of them require a return address. If you choose to use the methods that require a return address and don't mind sellers having your home address, then you don't need a virtual mailbox. However, if you are sensitive about your personal privacy, a mailbox is a necessary expense. And let me tell you, sometimes you will contact some very angry people.

There are a few ways you could rent a mailbox. I recommend a virtual mailbox because many of them will take pictures of your mail and email it to you. Anytimemailbox is absolutely amazing because they even have an app.

The plans start at $9.99/month. It doesn't matter if you choose a city that is near you or not, just pick the cheapest one you can find. There may be a small fee for forwarding or scanning mail, but each mailbox includes different services in the base price so you could save some serious money just by shopping around. Once you start to do more deals, you might need to upgrade to a more expensive plan that includes free, unlimited forwarding or scanning, but for now, I honestly wouldn't expect more than 10 postcards in a single month unless you will be sending out several thousand mailers.

Some UPS stores have physical mailboxes for rent if you'd rather go with a physical location. The prices vary by store but are generally $150 every six months. That's 2.5x the price of anytimemailbox, and I am not impressed by the fact that I have to pick up my mail - even if it is free for an unlimited amount of postcards. If you are that worried, then you should just upgrade to a more expensive anytimemailbox plan.

In my opinion, Anytimemailbox is the best option to start - especially if you don't have $150 upfront. To sign up for anytimemailbox, go to mail.beauxblast.com.

Low Costs: $10/month

High Costs: $25/month

A Cloud-Based Phone System

For virtually all marketing, you need a phone. You can use your personal number, but most real estate investors use a cloud-based system to protect their privacy, route calls to their assistants, and have a business-specific voicemail.

I recommend RingCentral.com. For $34.99/month, you get their standard plan, which has 1000 minutes, unlimited texting, several lines, and much more. You can download the app on both iPhone and Android, so it will work for 99% of you.

If you are very low on cash, Google Voice gives you most of the same benefits for free. However, if you use it for texting or voice campaigns, potential sellers can block you, and Google will penalize you by turning off your service. Usually, it is only for a few hours, but if you get blocked enough, they will turn it off permanently. Your phone number is going to be on all your mailers so it's best if you can keep the same one permanently.

Low Costs: $0

High Costs: $34.99/month

Section 3: Unnecessary Startup Costs

A Website

Huh? Don't you think a website is necessary?

No, I don't... er well, it's complicated. Let me start by explaining the two different types of websites. The first type of website is a vanity site. This is just a little website you put on your business card or send to your potential sellers to let them know you are a legitimate business. It seems everyone and their gramma has a vanity website nowadays ...and they do help immensely with credibility. If you have the money for it, it's a great buy but completely unnecessary.

The second type of website is a ranking website. These sites rank on the first page of google and are what you would see when you search for a certain keyword phrase, like "Buy my land Utah". You generally use this kind of site to make your company accessible to people trying to sell their land.

What's the difference between the two types of websites? Thousands of dollars and months of work... the vanity site will not have external Search Engine Optimization, so it will be much cheaper to create and maintain. The ranking site will have external SEO, so it's going to be more expensive but also more useful for your business.

If you are just getting started and you are starting from $0, do not waste your time on a website. You will do fine without one because you'll be marketing in ways that only require a phone or an address.

If you are broke, you technically can create your own vanity website, but it will slow you down and take you away from actual money-making activities... plus, there is the additional cost of hosting each month. That is 20 bucks of your budget you could spend on literally anything else.

Now, if you are planning on using a ranking website as your main source of marketing, that's a different story. To do this, you will either need a few thousand dollars OR a lot of time. I can't effectively explain SEO here, but you can visit seo.beauxblast.com to learn from experts. Keep in mind, this method is very time-consuming in the beginning and could take months to get up and running... but it is doable.

If you have a bit of money and want to invest in a website, then I have a great recommendation for you - Scalable Real Estate Investment Websites. You can find them at website.beauxblast.com. They can build you either a vanity site or a ranking site. It's hard to tell you exactly what you will pay because they operate on a sliding scale determined by your investment location and website needs, however, I did manage to work out a deal with them for anyone who mentions my book. They will build your website for 25% off and give you one month of hosting for free.

If you want them to build and host a vanity site, it will be around $250 to build and $40/month to host. If you want a ranking site, it starts at $250 per month. Usually, land investing keywords are not that competitive, so it should be cheaper.

If you want to make the website yourself, be prepared to learn everything about SEO, and work for several months before you get a lead. You will need to write all the copy, get all the pictures, and do all the SEO. You have two options for this as well - you can either learn how to use WordPress or Carrot. Both have their advantages and disadvantages.

Wordpress is decidedly cheaper because you do everything yourself. You need to figure out how to use Wordpress, how to host your website, and how to purchase templates. The hosting fees for Wordpress can be as low as $4/month, so if you have patience and are technically savvy, this may be a good route for you. Go to wordpress.com to get started.

If you want something that is more "done for you", you can use Carrot. With Carrot, you will have a website up and running in a matter of minutes. However, their hosting fees start at $50/month, so you pay for that convenience. If you plan on creating a ranking site, they have a lot of free resources that can help you through creating it. Go to seo.beauxblast.com for a free introduction on how to get started. It's not a walk in the park. You'll still need to find backlinks, write your own copy, and create your own GoogleMyBusiness page but if you are still interested in using Carrot, go to carrot.beauxblast.com to get started.

There is a secret third way I want to mention - creating a Facebook business page. Some people use a Facebook business page as their website. I don't know that it works particularly well for real estate, but if you're seriously tight on funds, want a website, and have a few minutes, you can create one on Facebook. I describe how to create a Facebook business page in chapter 2, so hang on until then if this is the route you decide to go.

Make sure you keep in mind that you need two distinct websites. Why? You need to keep your buyers and sellers separate. You don't want your sellers to see what you're selling land for because they will raise their price. This would seriously eat into your profits and is well worth having two websites.

Low Costs: $0/month

High costs: $5000+/month

Setting Up Your LLC

LLCs are there to protect you from liability if something goes wrong. If you plan on renting out land, doing major updates, or holding it, then an LLC is something you need sooner rather than later. Unfortunately, many people are looking to make a quick buck on someone else's misfortune, and while most land investors never go to court, it can happen. LLCs protect you from being personally sued if you do "win the lottery" and end up in court.

You probably don't need a Limited Liability Company (LLC) until you complete a deal. It's a time consuming and frustrating experience that will put unnecessary stress on you while you get your business going.

The cost of getting an LLC will vary by state. The average cost in the United States is $100 if you file on your own and could be up to $1500 if you have a lawyer or a company file it for you. Ultimately, filing for an LLC is up to you and your risk tolerance. You should do it eventually (even if it's only for the tax advantages), but you probably don't need to do it before your first deal... not for land investing anyway.

Low Costs: $100+

High Costs: $1500+

Logo, Business Identity and Business Cards

Are they useful? Yes, they can be. Do they make you feel hella professional? You bet they do! Are they necessary? No, they are not! And, as a bonus, they are an excellent place for new investors to waste time.

Lots of new investors get hung up on creating their perfect logo or their ideal business card. I don't want that to be you. Success loves speed - so the more time you waste on things that are not directly helping you find leads, the more likely you are to give up. I don't want you to give up!

When you have done a few deals and want to make a business card, you should use VistaPrint. I use them for my business cards because I feel like they have a good price for decent quality. Go to vistaprint.com to get started.

Most investors have plain white cards with their name, number, email, and website. Your card doesn't need to be fancier than - no one will be impressed!

If you want someone to make your business card design for you, you can go to fiverr.com. Use a Level 2 seller. You will pay between $15 to $300 for a design and about $30 to get them printed.

Low Costs: $30

High costs: $330+

Accounting Software

I don't recommend you get any software or hire an accountant before you do 1 deal. Do keep track of your miles and receipts, though because an accountant will still be able to help retroactively.

The cheap, but more time-consuming bookkeeping method is to use QuickBooks. Quickbooks will save you several thousand dollars but is only as good as you are. A small business would only need to pay QuickBooks $25/month.

Most accountants ask for a startup fee and a monthly retainer. I'm not saying not to use an accountant, I'm just saying you don't need one right off the bat. It's a waste of your money to have them on retainer when you have nothing for them to do.

Low Costs: $25/month

High costs: $150+/month

TOTAL COST BREAKDOWN

Bare Minimum Startup Costs

Expense	Low Cost	High Cost
Education	$0	$5000+*
Lists	$0	$300+
Finding Investments	$0	$2000
Property Acquisition	$0**	$1000+
Holding Costs	$0	$1000+
Selling Costs	$200	$1000+
Contract Templates	$0	$39.99
Total Bare Minimum Startup Costs your first month	**$200**	**$10340**

Recommended Startup Costs

Expense	Low Cost	High Cost
Mailbox	$10	$250
Cloud Based Phone System	$0	$34.99
Total Recommended Startup Costs your first month	**$10**	**$285**

Unnecessary Startup Costs

Expense	Low Cost	High Cost
A Website	$0	$5000+
An LLC	$100+	$1500+
Logo, Business Identity, Business Cards	$30	$330
Accounting Software	$25	$150
Total Unnecessary Costs	**$155**	**$6980**

*You obviously will not be purchasing a new course every month (At least I hope not!) so you can likely subtract this from your usual expenses. ** This is a best-case scenario where you are either able to wholesale the property or find a seller who is willing to finance as well as a property that does not have any taxes or liens on it. You are more likely to need between $250 and $1000 for each property.*

2

HOW TO FIND THE MOST UNDERVALUED LAND

O k you think, *where do I find this cheap land? Does it just grow on trees?* Good question! And timely too because that's the topic of this chapter. I'm going to show you which areas are likely to have land for sale and exactly how to find it. Ready?

WHERE YOU SHOULD INVEST FOR INSANE ROIS

The goal is to find land where there is job growth, low crime, and a population under 100,000/square mile. Basically, we are investing in up-and-coming towns within 1-2 hours of major cities. We will be using a computer for most of the research, so make sure you have one handy. It works best if you follow along as you read and fill out the companion pdf you got when you signed up for my checklist bundle at the beginning of the book.

First, if you plan on closing without a title company, google which states allow a self close. It's probably easier to write a list of states to avoid than which states you should invest in. Once you have that list, Google which states allow owner financing. Owner financing is the primary strategy used by land investors to create passive income. You might read online that you, as an individual, can only owner finance once per year. While this is true for properties that have a structure on them, it is not true for raw land. You should be able to owner finance as many as you want without forming an LLC and applying for a license - but make sure you double-check by calling a title company, hiring a lawyer, or searching the internet.

Once you have a list of all the states that allow owner financing and self-closing, pick one in the midwest. You probably want to look at the flyover states first because the land is usually cheaper. Once you have your state, use google maps to look for big cities. Then, look for smaller towns that are approximately 60-120 miles away. Once you have a list of 10 potential towns, move on to the next step.

We will judge these towns by looking at three metrics: job growth, crime rate, and population. Luckily, we can find all this information in one place - bestplaces.net. Type in one of your potential investment towns or their associated zip code. Bestplaces will show you an overview of that town. On the left, you will see a table that is labeled "Categories". Open the Crime, Economy, and People stats tabs. Each of these will show you the associated information for that town compared to the national average.

Let's start with crime. We want to avoid high crime areas because it will make it harder to sell. At the top of the page, you should see two bold sentences telling you about violent crime and property crime. Next to those, it will tell you the US average. You want to make sure that both violent and property crime are below the national average. If they are, write that down. If they are not, skip to the next town.

Now, move on to the economy tab. The second paragraph should say something along the lines of "This town has seen the job market increase…".

Look for the prediction number for the next 10 years. That will give you the predicted job growth. Compare that with the national average, which should be in the same sentence. Make sure that the job growth for your town is greater. If it is not, start over with the next town on your list. If it is, make a note and move on to the people stats.

In the very first paragraph of people stats, there's a bolded sentence that tells you how many people per square mile. We want this to be under 100,000. If it isn't, start over with the next town. After you've done this for all of the towns you selected, pick out the three best. If you need to go to a different city or state, then do so. Don't cheat this step!

Great! Now you have three towns that look promising. Pat yourself on the back because that's a huge step in the right direction. However, we have a few more things to check before we start spending our hard-earned cash and limited time.

First, make sure that these areas have a GIS map online. This is a map that will show you the property lines around each property. Any property that you find needs to have its property lines verified by the GIS map. You can do this by searching <County Name> County Gis map. The next step depends on which method you choose for lead generation. If you choose to use lists as your main source of lead generation, check agentpro247.com for data freshness. I'll show you how to do this later on.

If you choose to invest without a listing service, you can check for foreclosure and tax-delinquent information for your investment county online. You can usually find that information here: https://www.biggerpockets.com/rei/real-estate-public-records/.
If it isn't there, you can also perform a google search. If you can't find it on Google, it's not online and you should likely move on.

There is no standard for what the foreclosure, probate, or tax-delinquent websites should be called, look like, or contain, so I can't tell you exactly how to use each website. You'll have to do a little looking and move on if it doesn't look promising for that town. This is where you are going to get most of your information, so the town you choose must have at least one of these resources. If you really want to invest in that county and they don't have their information online, you have to call the county clerk's office and ask them what their process is for giving this information - which is time-consuming and expensive. As I've said before, I recommend against this right now - but it is definitely something to look into after you are more established.

Action Item: Make sure you have at least 5 places that you want to invest in before continuing.

The next step is to determine the average price per acre for that county and find a local real estate agent who can tell us about the market. Warning - the next part attempts to guide you through a website. They do change, so bear with me here and pause if necessary.

Go to zillow.com. You can use Trulia or a similar tool, but my favorite tool for comping is Zillow. Put one of your counties into the search bar, and press enter. You should see a map of your area. Along the top, you will see "For Sale", "For Rent" or "Sold". Click on whichever one you see. Make sure you have "Sold" and "For Sale" checked. You can tell it's checked if the circle next to the word "Sold" has a blue dot. Click on "Price" and put $500 as the minimum. Leave the maximum blank. Leave Bed and Baths at Any.

Now click on "Home Type". Make sure that only Lots/Land is selected, then click the "Done" button.

Next, click on the blue "More" button. Scroll down and make sure that the "Sold in Last" dropdown is set to 12 months.

Look to the right side of the screen. At the top, you can click on the "Sort by" dropdown. I like to sort by price or lot size. Now you will see a list of all the lots, how big they are, where they are, and the price they are now or sold for recently. If you hover your mouse over the land, you will see exactly where this land is located.

If you see most land in that area is worth a bazillion dollars, chances are you will not be able to find land in your budget. For your first deal, we are looking for land that is around $10,000-$20,000. Why so low? Keep in mind, you will be selling the land for about 80% and buying for 10%-30% of the average price per acre. Once you've found an area that has property in your price range, use the following formula.

First...

Price of property / Number of acres in that property = price per acre.

Then...

(Add all Price per Acre numbers you found above) / Number of properties = Average Price per acre

You will base your offer and sales price on that calculation, so make sure you write it down. You should do this for all the counties that you are looking at to determine which one is your best bet. Remember, your price range is 10%-30% of the Average Price per Acre value that we found above.

Now, back to Zillow. Select a property and look at the details. The right side of the website will show you a list of realtors. You need to know how long you will hold this property. Call a few of the realtors and do the following.

- Tell them that you are an investor interested in raw or vacant land of xx acres.
- Ask them how long these properties generally take to sell in that area.
- Ask them what they think a good sales price might be to turn it around quickly.

Some of the realtors probably won't be able to help you because they don't deal with land, but some of them will. Take what they say and compare it with the average sales price you calculated earlier to give yourself a rough estimate of land value in this area. Generally, 70% of the average price per acre will turn a property around in no time, so use 70% of your estimate as the price you will sell for.

As a beginner, I would caution you not to invest in commercial land. Some of the environmental regulations for commercial land can really screw a new investor over. For instance, you don't know what business was there before, and you don't know what they've done to the land. If there are any environmental issues, it will make it nearly impossible to sell, and you will be responsible for fixing them. Residential or mixed purpose land is going to be the safest bet for you simply because you don't have to worry about past environmental hazards.

Action item: Find 3 areas near you in which you can invest

Finding Motivated Sellers

I want to pause for a moment and talk about your mindset.I promise - this isn't a pep talk book... but mindset is critical when you invest in anything. For instance - I'm sure you've heard the phrase buy low, sell high. Easy enough, right? Well, if you go into the stock market with the wrong mindset, you will end up buying high and selling low because you'll jump on the bandwagon late and sell when the market drops. You have to go into investing with a plan and then you need to stick to that plan.

There are two things that I want to warn you about before we start finding motivated sellers. First, some of the deals that you find will not be good enough, and that's ok! Sometimes the numbers just don't work out. The best thing you can do is let the deal go and pat yourself on the back for making progress!

The second point: some of the motivated sellers you talk to are going through a life crisis. Maybe they're about to lose their land and ruin their credit score. Maybe their parents just died and left them all their land. They probably don't know what to do with it and might even feel guilty selling it. You just don't know what these motivated sellers are going through, so make sure you always treat them with compassion.

With that out of the way, let's discuss a few different methods you can use to find motivated sellers. Do not try to use all of these methods at once because it will be overwhelming. I would advise you to pick 1 or 2 that you can afford and have time for and stick to those for six months. After you've done it for half a year, you can reevaluate.

Landhub.com/Landwatch.com

Time: Hours

Money: A fee when you sell

These websites are popular wholesaling sites for land investors. You can create a free buyer profile and start hunting for land deals immediately. They have it broken down under the "Property For Sale" dropdown menu. Keep in mind, you are not going to find crazy discounted land here because you are purchasing from a wholesaler. However, it is an easy way to find land for sale, and you will definitely be able to squeeze a profit out of a few deals. Note, you might need to negotiate with the seller - there's nothing wrong with that so don't be afraid!

Since you are starting out without a true mentor, purchasing some land from these sites is actually a really great first move! I'm not going to lie - talking to sellers can be horrible, especially when you aren't confident. One of the ways to gain that confidence is to do a few deals. Admittedly, finding a deal is the hardest part - so why not use an aggregation site first and then use one of the techniques I show you in chapter 5 to start generating income? Will your returns be crazy? No! But you will gain confidence and knowledge. And those are the keys to success. You will more than likely make a little money off it too.

My recommendation is to search for properties here first, do 2 or 3 deals to get your confidence up before you start leveraging other methods. It's kind of like a cheat code to confidence.

Tax Sales

I'm going to talk about this method early on because you need to know about it and you'll probably hear about it. If you are a beginner, I recommend that you read what I am about to tell you, mumble "Well, that's pretty complicated." and then move on to one of the other methods. If this method really strikes you for some reason, I recommend you read more targeted books.

When I talk about tax sales, I am talking about land that has made it through the entire delinquent tax process and is now in an auction. An important distinction I want to make is between tax sales and finding a tax delinquent property. Tax delinquent properties are NOT in the auction yet. They have

NOT been auctioned off yet. You have caught it BEFORE the tax sale.

A property is considered tax delinquent for a period of time BEFORE the tax sale. Purchasing one of these is different than purchasing one FROM a tax sale. For starters, it's a lot less complicated. This section is all about purchasing land from an auction, not saving the owner from the auction by purchasing a tax delinquent property. Confused? I hope not.

Tax sales are a great way to find properties. In fact, some investors solely use tax sales for their businesses. I just recommend you learn more about it before you jump into it because it's complicated.

Maybe you've heard you can find crazy deals at auctions. It's true, you can, but you probably haven't heard why. The land is cheap because the government only cares about collecting back taxes. If you look at an auction, you might see a situation where the land is worth $500,000, but the government only wants $10,000!

Dang! That sounds like a crazy deal!

And it is! But, as they say, if it's too good to be true, usually it is.

First of all, you need to pay the entire amount you bid in the tax sale the day of the sale. Also of note, this is an auction, so the price on the website is not the final price. You will be competing with other investors for this land! If you do manage to purchase some of the land, you still have to deal with the legal aspects of purchasing land that has previously defaulted on the government.

Laws governing the delinquent tax process are different in every state, but luckily I am here to give you 90% of the information you need to invest anywhere in the US. The properties that go to auction are way behind on their taxes - usually about 2-3 years. Each county has a different schedule for their auctions, so you need to use google to find out when they are and if they are online or in-person only. If you find a website, usually it will have all of the properties that are being auctioned off with descriptors and a starting bid.

There are two types of tax sales - Deed Auction and Lien Certificate Auction. A deed auction sells the actual deed for the property - you pay what the previous owner owed the government and then immediately own it. Simple right? But there's a catch.

If there are any other liens on the property, you may be liable for paying them off or for paying a title company to clear them. This is an expensive process that could cost tens of thousands of dollars. Second, you do not own the title. This is rather important because it means you will have to spend more money trying to obtain a clear title. You can do this in two ways, Action to Quiet Title or a Title Certificate. I won't go too into detail about these techniques because if you find yourself needing to do this, you will likely have a lawyer on your team. Keep in mind that it will be at least $1000 and a month of waiting.

A Lien Certificate is a little different than a deed. With Lien certificates, you are purchasing a lien on the property. As the owner of this lien, you have a mortgage on the land. That means the owner has a certain amount of time to pay off the lien before you can foreclose. This waiting period is called a redemption period and is different for each redemption state. Redemption periods can be as little as 60 days or as much as four years. The maximum interest rate you are allowed to charge the property owner is also determined by the state but it is somewhere between 5% and 26%.

By the end of the redemption period, the owner will either pay you what they owe you or forfeit their land. It's complicated, expensive, and time-consuming, but it is a strategy used by many land investors to make a lot of money. Once you have a few deals under your belt and have a relationship with a title company and a lawyer, you may want to give this a try! However, this is just the CliffsNotes, and I would read a few more books on it first if that is the direction you choose.

CONTACTING SELLERS DIRECTLY

Facebook Marketplace

Time: A few times a day for a few minutes

Money: Free

If you don't have a Facebook account, create one! The only way you can use Facebook Marketplace is if you have a Facebook account. You can use Facebook Marketplace to look for land that is For Sale By Owner (FSBO). Search for "Land", "Land for Sale", etc to see what comes up. Contact each of these sellers with an offer.

Zillow

Time: Once a day for a few minutes

Money: Free

Search for "Zillow FSBO <county>" in google. Follow the same steps as earlier so that only land is showing. Contact each of these sellers with an offer.

Redfin

Time: Once a day for a few minutes

Money: Free

Redfin is an app where you can sell properties without paying the full agent fee. To use redfin, you download the app and create an account. Tap on the "Filters" button and make sure that everything is blank. Go to property type. Deselect everything except for "Land". Now, look around. Adjust the filters as is necessary. Select a few that you think look great and start making offers!

Note: A good strategy is to make offers on land that has been on the market for more than 90 days. The sellers are usually more desperate by then, and the longer land has been on the market, the more they want to sell it.

5Miles app

Time: Once a day for a few minutes

Money: Free

This app is a lot like Facebook marketplace. Use it in the same way.

Craigslist.com

Time: Once a day for a few minutes

Money: Free

Craigslist is a website marketplace where anonymous buyers sell to anonymous sellers. Go to craigslist.com. Once there, in the search bar on top the left, type in "<your city> land for sale".

Driving for Dollars

Time: Hours

Money: The price of Gas

This is when you drive around looking for land that might be for sale. A good indication that land is for sale is when the land has a billboard saying "for sale". You can call every number, learn about the land, and make an offer! This only works if you are trying to invest near where you live.

Using a Real Estate Agent

Time: Once a day for a few minutes

Money: 10% of purchase/sale price

Not all Real Estate Agents are investor-friendly. However, being honest and upfront about your goals is always the best policy. Ask them if they would be willing to set you up on a daily drip with the MLS so long as you use them to purchase the land you find there. Let them know that you will be making very low offers, and if they are not ok with that, you should amicably end your business arrangement. There are many realtors out there, and it's important to find one you can work with. I showed you how to find them on Zillow earlier, so if you are interested in using a realtor, you can find some there.

Sometimes, realtors come across properties before anyone else, and you want them to think of you first! They will also run comps for you on land that you are interested in purchasing through them.

When you ask for an MLS drip, ask for land properties that have been around for 60 days+ or are expired. Also, ask for properties that have experienced a price drop. Usually, realtors can only work in certain zip codes. You should ask them for all the zipcodes they are clear to work in. If you do find some land on the MLS, leverage the realtor to do some of your work for you - ask your realtor to run comps and do some of the due diligence.

MLS properties can be found! Some investors only use MLS. It is up to you to pick out the good and the bad. Keep in mind that you will be paying a fee each time you purchase a property! (But not necessarily sell it since there are other places to sell!) Another thing to remember is that MLS deals are not as discounted as FSBO.

Using AgentPro247's Lists

Time: 30 minutes

Money: subscription fee $30 + $.05 / lead

Go to AgentPro247.com. When you sign up, you can select which of the packages you would like. I base the above price on the cheapest one. I am not affiliated with AgentPro247.com, I just think they have the most to offer. Warning: This is an attempt to guide you through the process of using this listing service. Make sure you purchase an account before you proceed.

Once you log in, you should see a screen with a graphic FARM on the left and a map in the middle.

Above that map, there is a button that says "Tools". Click on that and then click on Geographic Coverage. Now click on the state you are investing in.

Voila! A spreadsheet should pop up on the right. Remember when I said that you should check AgentPro247 to see how fresh the data is? Well, this is how you do that. From now on, when you research a new county, do this as part of that research. The freshness spreadsheet includes the state, county, what is included, and how current the data is. Make sure the counties you select have data in Agentpro247 that has been sourced within the last two months. If none of them are at least that fresh, you need to select different counties. Luckily, this will take you even less time than before because now you know all of the steps. One way you could speed up the process is by making a list of the fresh counties and checking those against your crime/population/city etc. criteria.

Once you have some counties that fit the freshness criteria as well as the crime, population, and city criteria, go back to the previous page, select your state, and type each county in the top search bar. Click on Property Use & Characteristics. On property types, select Recreational, Residential Vacant Land, and Agricultural/Rural. Click ok.

Scroll down to "Lot Size". I would start at 1 acre and up. Make sure you select "Acres" in "Lot Size Unit". Now select Absentee. This means that the owner of the land does not live in the state. We want to target the absentee owners because they are more likely paying for land they don't use and therefore they are not as emotionally attached.

If you want to close with a title company, you can skip this paragraph. Scroll down to "Owner Type". Select it. At the bottom of the dropdown, there are two radio buttons - Include, Exclude. Select Exclude and select all. Click Ok. This excludes all of the land owned by trusts. It can be hard to find the trust owner if you do not use a title company, so this will save you a lot of headaches later on.

Now, go to Sale, Assessed & Phones. Under Distressed, you will see Foreclosure and Tax. Select those if you'd like. It will narrow your search to people who are in foreclosure and going through tax sales. I'd leave them blank for now.

Now, scroll down to % Improvement. Put in 0-0. We do this because we do not want any structures on the land. Select which range of values you'd like to include in Market Value. I would recommend you have at least $500 in there.

Click on the "Count Only" button. You may need to change some of the filters to get more people on your list. If you see on the right that you have "Count:0" then change some of the filters to broaden your search. There is an infinite number of ways you can filter your list.

Make sure you have the number of people you want to contact on the right and then click on "View Records". This will allow you to look at the information before you download it. You can scroll through it and remove any properties or duplicates that do not look like they fit your criteria. You should also take out any of the "No Address.". You will only have to do this one time for this list, and it will save you money, so do it.

Click select records and name your list. An Export Button should have appeared. Click Export and then select all Elements. Open up the CSV file in your favorite type of table analysis program. It could be excel, numbers, or google sheets.

There are several ways you can market using these

lists. All of them will get the job done - the important thing is that you select one and stick with it. Read on to see which one is right for you!

Mail Campaigns

Time: 20 minutes

Cash: ~$.50 / lead

A mail campaign is exactly what it sounds like - we will be mailing all of the motivated sellers that we found from Agentpro247 and ask them if they would consider selling. To do this, we have to format our list and upload it to a mailing service.

To format your list, save a copy of the original list. You will need all the information in the original later on when you speak with the seller.

In the new sheet, delete all of the columns except "Owner Name Formatted", "Mail Address", "MCity", "MState", "MZip", "MUnit Type", and "MUnit Number". Make sure they appear in that order. Copy the information in the MUnit Number and concatenate it to the information in the MUnit Type column. Delete the 7th column when you are done.

Now rename all your columns as shown below:

- "Name" - instead of Owner Name Formatted
- "Address" - instead of Mail Address
- "City" - instead of MCity
- "State" - instead of Mstate
- "Zipcode" - instead of MZip
- "Unit" - instead of MUnit Type

Go through your list again and delete duplicate information. Some owners may have more than one property and will be in there twice. If you keep the duplicates in there, they will get 2 postcards. Don't waste your money - they only need 1.

Save your file in excel format.

Now we are going to upload this list into a mailing service. Trust me, if you want to do mailers, you do not want to do it from your living room. It is cheaper to use a Direct Mail company, and it will save you your sanity.

I have found that click2mail.com has the best bang for your buck, so we're going to use them for all of our campaigns. We will be sending out yellow postcards for a variety of reasons. 1) They are pretty damn cheap if not the cheapest. 2) They look like a warning from the government so they will catch your motivated seller's attention. 3) The words are on the outside, so they have to read it as they are throwing it away. If you send a letter out, they will think it's junk and automatically toss it.

Go to click2mail.com now.

If you've chosen to do mailers, keep reading because this section describes creating an order! If not, feel free to skip.

Still here? Alright! Let's make your first order!

Make sure your account is created before you proceed or the rest of the chapter won't make sense to you. Once you are ready, go to Mail & Print Products at the top. Select the 4.5x6 postcard. The price changes based upon how many you buy, but generally it's around or under 50 cents per postcard.

Click on the yellow "Start Here" button. You can get the exact price here before you start your order. Once you are satisfied, click on "Start Job". This brings you to the page where you can configure your postcard. Make sure…

- The address is correct
- The layout is double-sided
- Production time is next day
- Print color is Black and White

- Paper type is Yellow
- Mail class is first class.

Once you have all of that done, click on "Select/Upload". Here, we will create the copy for our postcards. Click on 'Create Document". Either you can create the document here, or you can upload one. I like to create it here so I know it looks right.

You can put anything you want on this postcard, but the general message should always be the same.

> *Attention { Name }!*
> *My name is Beaux, and I am interested in purchasing your land. If you have considered selling for any reason, you should call me right away. I will buy it as-is and make it simple, fast, and easy for you to turn your land into cash. If you're interested, give me a call at 555-555-5555.*
> *I hope to talk soon!*
> *Beaux*

Of course, you should add your own name and phone number in there instead of mine. As for the { Name }, this is some code that the website uses to add each motivated seller's name to their own post-card. It makes it much more personal and it's super easy - just select "Name" in the top-left dropdown.

Then, select continue. The page will scroll down to the bottom where you should select "Upload a new list". Select your list and upload it.

Now, you should be on a screen where you need to map the columns from your excel sheet to the fields on the website. Put "Name" as recipient Lines. Address for Address Lines. Select "Add line" and put Unit there. City/Town, State/Province, and Zip/Postal code go in their designated spots as well. Now click "Save and Close". It should be pretty self-explanatory - just don't overthink it.

You can add yourself to the list here by clicking on "Select Add myself to the list". This will let you know when your postcards are out. Select Continue. This should bring you to an area where you can look at your final product. Make sure your postcards are exactly as you want them because once you are done, they will be mailed. When you're satisfied, add it to your cart and get ready to have some calls coming in!

There are a few different philosophies on how often

you should send postcards out. I think that once a month for 6 months is a great strategy because the motivated seller may not have seen your postcard before or it might have been a bad time for them. You will probably receive some postcards with "could not deliver" stamped on them. Just take those addresses out of click2mail so you don't spend any more money on bum addresses.

If you are using the foreclosure list, you probably only have one month to send these out because the properties will be foreclosed on by the time your second mailer reaches them. In that case, you should send a letter every week up to the sale.

If you are mailing to the tax delinquent list, you may have a little more time depending on the county's tax sale date. Make sure you know when the property will go off the market due to either tax or foreclosure sale before you send your mail. If you continue sending it after the sales, you are wasting money.

Cold Calling

Time: 10 cold calls/hour

Money: $0.15/lead

Another strategy is cold calling. It is exactly what it

sounds like, you get a phone number for each lead and then give them a call. If they pick up, you ask them if they are ready to sell their property. If they don't pick up, you leave a nice message. If the number is disconnected, you add their name to a list where you can either use one of the other marketing strategies to contact them or use a more expensive skip tracing service.

If you want to use cold calling, then keep reading! If not, feel free to skip this section.

The first step is to get your list skip traced. I recommend starting with reiskip.com. It's going to be about $.15 per skip trace, so it is very affordable, and it's one of the better affordable skip tracing services out there. Expect to receive a list with 50%-70% of the numbers filled in. That is not bad for $0.15 per lead! Go to reiskip.com now and create an account. I will show you how to use it in the following section.

Once you verify your email, you should be taken to a place where you can either skip trace a single person or skip trace a list. You want to skip trace a list.

Enter your payment information and then upload your list. Much like before, you will have to enter the column names into the appropriate places. The remaining steps are self-explanatory.

In a few days, you will get back a list of phone numbers and names. Now, it is up to you to give each phone number a call. There are some call services out there that will autodial for you, but I have never used one so I don't have any recommendations. If you want to use one, expect to pay between $50 and $150/month.

When you start calling, three things can happen. One, they could answer. If they answer, you should respond pleasantly:

> *Hi - name!*
> *My name is Beaux. I am interested in*
>   *buying your land on <street>. Have you*
>   *considered selling it?*

Two, you could get a voicemail. In that case you should have a script written. Say the same script every time, try not to tweak it.

> *Hi - name!*
> *My name is Beaux and I am interested in*
>   *purchasing your land. If you have*

> *considered selling for any reason, you*
> *should call me back right away. I will*
> *buy it as-is and make it simple, fast,*
> *and easy for you to turn your land into*
> *cash. If you're interested, give me a call*
> *at 555-555-5555.*
> *I hope to talk soon!*
> *Beaux*

Three, you could get a disconnected or wrong number. This happens sometimes - just make a note of it and either skip this number or add it to your list of potential sellers that need to be skip traced by a more expensive service or added to another type of marketing (like mailers).

A note on skip tracing - the more expensive the service, the more accurate the information. Different services have different levels of clearance into sensitive information. Some of the more expensive skip trace services (a few dollars per name) will get you very accurate information. We don't really need that right now, though. The numbers you get from reiskip are fine for our purposes because we are not operating in competitive markets.

Texting

Time: ~60/hour

Money: ~$.15/lead

Texting is very similar to cold calling - it just takes less time! I personally like texting more than cold calling because I get a better response rate and it's about 10x faster. Some investors do not like it because they think it is unprofessional. To them I say, get with the times! But, I leave it up to you to decide.

To get their numbers, you will need to use the same strategy for skip tracing we used in the cold calling section. We will also use very similar messaging. In fact, when I did cold call people, I would often text them immediately after leaving a message. Some people just prefer to look at a text than a voicemail!

I usually use a variation of the following message when I text them:

> *Hi - name!*
> *My name is Beaux and I am interested in purchasing your land. If you have considered selling for any reason, you should contact me right away. I will buy it as is and make it simple, fast,*

and easy for you to turn your land into
cash. If you're interested, shoot me a
text.
I hope to talk soon!
Beaux

Sometimes, the texters will ask how you found their number. My answer is always, "I happened to find you through public records. Amazing what you can find online these days!".

Note: You will have to look into your own state's laws for specifics, but in the United States, it is illegal to have a robot autotext. Autotexting is defined as a non-human sending texts out to people who did not consent to you texting them. So, that means you at least need to push 1 button for each unique text. If you send 10 at one time, that's illegal (unless they have consented to you texting them). If you send 1 at a time, that's legal, even if a non-human entity populated the text for you. Make sure you do not do anything illegal!

If you have a list of targeted numbers. You can find some programs online that speed up texting a list, but I haven't used them because the cheapest I found was too expensive for how long it takes to copy and paste a text. (About 10 seconds). If you have a mac, you can text them directly from your mac… but even if you just have a phone, it isn't that bad. Give it a try with your friends.

Facebook Ads

Time: 20 minutes

Money: It depends, but normally less than $200

Ah, Facebook ads. It's the newest way of asking people if they would like to sell. Unfortunately, there are a lot of intricacies with Facebook. In fact, there are hundreds of books, videos, and articles on it. You could spend months learning about Facebook ads and still not know everything. This book is not about Facebook ads, but I will give you the basics of what works for land investing so that you know how to get started using Facebook. After all, the basics aren't that hard and oftentimes you learn more on the job than reading from a book anyway!

One thing I'd like to mention is if you choose to use Facebook to advertise, you will probably need a website. I suggest you create a website on carrot (carrot.beauxblast.com) or WordPress. If you aren't technical at all, you can have it done for you by Scalable REI (website.beauxblast.com). In fact, if you wanted to pay someone to set up your Facebook ads, I believe they do that too.

When you set up social media marketing, you don't need a full SEO website - you just need a professional online presence. A vanity website still gives you credibility and credibility will help your leads on Facebook decide that they can trust you.

We will be doing simple Lead ads, so you will need a picture to capture people's attention. If you have a picture that would work well with your Facebook ad, then use that! If you don't, there are a lot of free rights picture websites. My personal favorite is pexels.com.

Choosing which picture is a personal choice. I like to go with pictures that have cute animals in them because those get me the most clicks. In general, your pictures should be related to money, land, or something eye-catching.

Before we can make any ads, we need to create a Facebook business page. Don't worry - it's really simple to do and you don't need an LLC.

Step 1. Create your Business Page

The first step is figuring out what people will call

you. Select a business name. It can be anything, but make sure it sounds professional. Do a quick google search to see if anyone else is doing business under that name before you settle on it. Avoid anything that says "Realty" because this word is reserved for realtors.

Go to facebook.com/pages/create. Select Business or Brand, enter your information, and select Real Estate as your Category. Fill in your information and click continue.

Now, upload a profile and cover image photo. They can be some of the ones you found online, a picture of yourself, or anything. It doesn't really matter as long as your page looks like a Real Estate Investing page. You want to make sure that your page looks professional because people will look at it. That being said, do not stress about it being perfect.

Now, create your username. Click Create Page @Username in the left menu. Click create username when you're done. Now, follow the prompts to add details about your business.

When you have completed all of the recommended steps, publish your page. That's it for step 1! You do not have to invite anyone if you don't want to. I know I didn't want to invite anyone to my page when I first created it because I didn't want to seem spammy to my friends and family. I strictly used the Facebook business page to create ads.

Step 2. Make some ads!

Log into Facebook ads manager at facebook.com/adsmanager. We are going to create a "Lead Generation" campaign that encourages people to give you their information so you can contact them.

Make sure your ad blocker is off if you have one. Now, go into the three-lined menu at the top left of the screen. Select "Payment Method" and enter in your preferred payment method. Once that is done, go back to the Ads Manager.

Step 2b. Create a new Campaign

Click the green create button and then click "Create New Campaign". Since we are in Real Estate, Facebook will most likely make you select "I'm creating a campaign for ads in a Special Ad Category". Go ahead and check this box and make sure the drop-down says "Housing". This will limit how we select our audience, but it won't hamper us too much. Now, select "Lead Generation" at the bottom under "What's your marketing objective?". Name your campaign and turn on "Campaign Budget Optimization". If you found more than one picture or have more than one ad message, you should do A/B testing. When you do A/B testing, make sure you only change 1 thing in the ad, or you won't know what caused your leads to like one ad over the other.

Set your budget to "Lifetime Budget" and put in a $5 lifetime budget. I like to start low, especially if I am A/B testing, because I want to see if the ad is effective. If you select "More options" you can further control how greedy or lax Facebook is with your money. You should check on your ads every day to examine and tweak them based on the results.

Add all of the following into interests - Agriculture, Building, Buy to let, Cash out Refinancing, Construction, Estate (land), Estate agent, For sale by Owner, General Contractor, Home Construction, Land, Land and Houses, Land lot, Landed property, Landlord, Manufactured Housing, Mobile Home, Prefabricated Home, Premier Agent - Zillow & Trulia, Property, Real Estate, Real Estate Agent Directory, Real Estate Appraisal, Real estate broker, Real estate development, real estate entrepreneur, Real estate investing, Real estate investment club,

Real estate investment trust, realtor.com, Realtor.com Pro, Renovation, Rent-to-own, Zillow.

All of the above are categories that people who own vacant land might be a part of. Since we are extremely limited on what we can do due to facebook's rules, we have to cast a wide net. But that's ok! Because the wider the net we cast, the cheaper our impressions will be. Impressions are defined as people who see your ad. Usually, it's about 2 cents per impression for me.

Select the desired schedule - I usually try an ad campaign for 2 days to see what kind of response it gets. Select Single image or video.

The headline should be:

Got Land? Thinking of selling?

The description should be

We buy land as is! Message me now for an instant, no obligations offer and turn your land into cash! 555-555-5555

I find that simple, enticing messages are often the best, but if you're great at copywriting, you can write as much as you like. If you aren't great at copywriting, you can head over to Fiverr and have them create some ads for you. It should only cost about $10. In my experience, using a level 2 seller is 100% worth it.

Edit the automatic messages along the side. Make sure there is nothing about an agent in there. I usually go with "Tell me more!" or "I'd like to sell my land!". Once you are done detailing your ad, click "Confirm!".

If, for some reason, Facebook tells you that you are violating their terms and services agreement, stop immediately and figure out what you are doing wrong. You do not want to be on the wrong side of Facebook!

If you are confused or stuck, there are a lot of videos online that show you how to set up Facebook ads. Fortunately, they will probably be more up-to-date than I can keep this book anyway. The important facet of this section is who you should be marketing to and that you can market to a custom audience eventually.

If you aren't technical and have the money for it, you can always head over to website.beauxblast.com for some help from Scalable REI websites.

Websites

Time: 3 months

Money: $8/month(wordpress) to $5000/month(Very competitive keywords with a pro)

One great advantage of websites is that motivated sellers come to you. That means they find your website online and enter in their own information with no active outreach from you at all. It is, by far, the least time-intensive method of advertising AFTER you get your website up and running. Most other methods of advertising take a lot of your time and money consistently. With websites, there's a pretty high startup cost, but after that, it's basically free.

Online lead generation (AKA, using a Search Engine Optimized website) is an excellent strategy that a lot of real estate investors choose to focus on, but that means it can be competitive. Unfortunately, I can't go too much into how to determine if the keywords you choose have a lot of competition, but there are many ways to figure that out. You can start by going to seo.beauxblast.com for a free introduction into

SEO. If a lead generation website is something you are seriously considering, it does come with some considerable costs.

Some of the major downsides are that you either have to spend time learning about SEO or hire someone to do it for you for a monthly fee. Fortunately, after a company gets you set up, you can stop paying them to do your SEO. However, proceed with caution because some of those companies will strip out the SEO when you stop paying them. Scalable REI Websites, the company I recommended in Chapter 1, will get you set up and will not strip out all of the SEO if you choose to discontinue their services. The worst they will do is offer to manage your website for a nominal fee every month and release it to you if you decline. If you have a few thousand dollars that you have earmarked for marketing, getting your website set up will pay in dividends. For instance, you can target the towns that you want to invest in, and then your website will pretty much be up there forever. If anyone in that town becomes interested in selling their land, they will see your website and give you a call.

If you choose to use websites, you will need one website for buyers and one for sellers. You can have as many buyer websites as you want targeting different areas around the United States, but it's best to keep all of the land you are trying to sell in one place because people will find your website and start looking through your inventory. There's no need to have your selling site separated into individual state websites. You should have a buying website and a selling website so your buyers do not try to use the prices on your selling website to negotiate with you. You want to offer the lowest fair amount. Giving them a bargaining chip will not help you.

That said, if you just want a vanity website you can point your buyers and sellers to, you can do it yourself using WordPress, or using carrot.beauxblast.com or you can have a professional do it for you by going to website.beauxblast.com. They do not need to be Search Engine Optimised because your goal is credibility. They just need to be online so you can direct people to them. SEO is only required if you are using the sites as part of lead generation.

Like I said earlier, lists and traditional marketing are less expensive to start up and easier to understand than online marketing. Traditional marketing also lends itself to you doing most of the work yourself, so it's cheaper. How you want to run your business is completely up to you, so make sure you select the method that makes the most sense to you. After all, not everyone is cut out to cold call and not everyone is technically savvy enough to create a website. We all need to play to our strengths.

Action Item: Use one or several of the above methods to find a list of motivated sellers

3

HOW TO NOT GET SCREWED

Due diligence is a critical step when investing in any property. You need to know the good, the bad, and the ugly before deciding to put any money into a deal. The good news is, most of the information you need to make an informed decision is either available for free online, from the Agent-Pro247 listing service, or a quick phone call away. It should only take about 15-20 minutes to do a pretty thorough investigation of any land deal. You should only do this for the properties after the motivated seller responds positively to your marketing(or after you've found a particularly great deal on landwatch.-com/landhub.com)!

Here is a list of the things that we will need to complete our due diligence.

	Owner	AgentPro/County	Other
The Legal Description		X	
The property size		X	
Are there access roads	X	X	
Is there water access	X		Utility Company
Is there electricity access	X		Utility Company
Is there gas access	X		Utility Company
Is there phone access	X		Utility Company
Is there Sewage	X		Utility Company
What is the zoning? Are there any restrictions?		X	
Is there an HOA?	X		
What is the Annual Tax Obligation?	X	X	
Is it within a flood zone?	X		msc.fema.gov/portal/search
Are there wetlands?	X		fws.gov/wetlands/data/Mapper.html
Has there been a percolation test recently?	X		
Can you see the parcel map?		X	
Are there any buildings, structures, or junk on the property?	X		google.com/maps OR hire someone on craigslist.com
What do the properties near it look like? Are they desirable?	X		google.com/maps OR hire someone on craigslist.com
Latitude and Longitude		X	
Outstanding Taxes, HOA or Liens	X	X	

Once we have all of the above information, we will run some comparables or "comps". One thing to keep in mind, especially with land, is you never truly know what a property is worth. What you need to realize is it doesn't matter what the land is really worth. The only thing that matters is how much it can sell for. Luckily, I'm going to teach you how to figure that out.

What Information can I get from the Seller

When a motivated seller contacts you, you need to collect some information from them. The goal of the first conversation is to collect information and give them a time frame that you will call them back with an offer. You can find a worksheet in the packet you downloaded at the beginning of the book. It's just easier to have you download a pdf than try to copy and print it here.

When you are speaking with them, make sure you know their name. You need it to search through the spreadsheet we got earlier from Agentpro247 and talk to them in conversation. Make sure you ask for the address of the land as well. Once you have their name and the address of the property in question, you can move on.

Now, ask them if they know what utilities are available on or near the land. (water, electricity, gas, sewage, phone.) You should also ask if they are using city water or well water. Septic or sewage (Or if they ever had a percolation test). We have other ways of figuring out the answers to those questions, but it's easier if they can answer you right then.

Ask them about road access. Is there a road connected to the property? Or do they have to go through someone else's property to get to their land? If they have to go through other property, ask if they legally own the driveway or if they have a handshake agreement with the other property owner. If they are relying on their neighbor's goodwill, you probably have to convince the neighbor to sell you the land that the driveway is on.

Ask them if there is an HOA on the land and what the fee is.

Ask them what they think they paid in taxes and if they owe anything.

Ask them if there are any structures on the land or if it is raw. Remember, in most owner financing friendly states, you can owner finance an unlimited amount of properties as long as it is considered raw land.

Never end the conversation without asking why they are selling. You want to figure out what pain the property is causing them. Feel free to lengthen the conversation with small talk about them, their land, and their problems because it increases rapport which makes them feel more comfortable and actually like you. The more they like you, the better chance they will do a deal. If you suck at building rapport, don't worry! You will get better in time. I found the secret for me was to be chatty and fill the silence with funny stories. Ask the seller a question, listen to their answer in full, and then tell a short, funny story.

And don't lie to the sellers! You want to be genuine and pleasant because this is as much about making them feel comfortable with you as it is about buying land.

Give them a timeline for the offer and make sure you have a way to reach them. If it's your first time talking with a motivated seller, tell them you will get back to them the next day. You want to give yourself plenty of time to do research.

Here is a list of all of the information you should have from them:

- Name
- Address
- A good number to reach them

- Pain points/Why are they interested in selling
- Road Access. What kind? A street or neighbor?
- Utilities (Water, gas, electric, sewage, phone)
- Type of water. City, well
- Type of sewage. City, septic, percolation test
- HOA
- Outstanding Taxes, Hoa fees, and liens
- Tax bill
- Are there any structures

FINDING INFORMATION ONLINE

From AgentPro247 or the County

If you chose to use Agentpro247 to find leads, you should also use Agentpro247 to perform due diligence. On the homepage, you can put in either the address or the owner's name and location. A dropdown on the left will let you select either address or owner name/location. Red pins will show up on the map so that you can choose the correct property. Or you can click on the address at the bottom of the page. Hover over whichever method you choose and click "reports".

You can select a lot of different information, but the best thing to do is to let the standard Property Profile come up. As you use this tool more, you might find that you have a different preference.

Here are the things you should be able to get from the report:

- APN
- Legal Description
- Zoning
- Assessment and Tax Information
- Latitude and Longitude of property
- Plat Map (The assessor's parcel map) - This shows you road access
- Outstanding Taxes, Liens, and HOA fees
- Transaction history - while not needed, it is still pretty helpful to see what it sold for last time.

After you have this report, there will only be a few things left to collect. If you are doing your first deal through landwatch/landhub or using any other method besides AgentPro247, you can find all of the information online or by calling the local county clerk's office - it's just a little more work.

Many counties have their information online. You can find most of their websites by going to https://www.biggerpockets.com/rei/real-estate-public-records/ and following the path. Usually, the county websites allow you to search for properties by owner name. If you can't find the website for your county, you need to call that county clerk's office and get the information from them over the phone.

Now that you have all of that information, let's move on to the rest of our due diligence.

Utilities

If the owner of the property doesn't know which utilities are connected or if you just want to double-check, you can google the county's local utility company and call them. If your property is in an area that is subdivided, i.e. has roads going through it, it probably has all of the utilities it needs. If it's your first time, I'd suggest calling the utility company because they will give you a definitive answer. They can also give you a quote on how much it will cost if the utilities need to be brought in. This is important because it will affect your resale value if other properties have utilities, and yours does not!

HOA

Many land investors stay away from land with an HOA because it restricts what you can do. Don't automatically throw out a deal if it has an HOA, just make sure you check with the realtors in that area to see if that property is still marketable.

Call the HOA to determine what the fees and restrictions are. If they can email you a copy of their bylaws, that's even better. Usually, unless the property is in a good neighborhood in a desirable location, it will be hard to sell. Most people who want to own large amounts of land want freedom. HOAs restrict freedom because they add more rules. They also charge a fee each month for the privilege of being part of an HOA. Make sure you know what that is because it will be part of your holding costs.

HOAs can also limit your ability to subdivide the land, so if that is your exit strategy, make sure it's still possible. The bottom line: don't automatically deny a property with an HOA, but make sure you proceed with caution!

OTHER INFORMATION

Flood Zone

A Flood zone is a place that the local government believes is at risk of flooding every 100 or 500 years. This makes the property less desirable for a number of reasons. First, if there is any part of your property in a flood zone, it will raise the insurance price. This makes it more expensive for the buyer because they will have to pay higher insurance. If you are planning on selling the property to someone who will build on it, it also limits where they can build because you generally can't build within a flood zone.

A flood zone can change a waterfront property from a great deal that will allow the buyer to build right on the lake to an ok deal because your buyer has to build their property a few acres away. With land, a flood zone is not a dealbreaker, but if you buy land with a flood zone, you will have to make sure you can still build a house in a desirable location (or sell to rice farmers!). You should also make sure it is typical for land in that area to be in a flood zone and accepted by the locals.

For example beaches and lakefront properties often

have flood zones. However, a random farm in the midwest or a lot in the middle of a landlocked city... probably not such a great idea. You should call an insurance company to see what the rates would be and maybe ask a local realtor what they think.

You can check if any property is in a flood zone using msc.fema.gov/portal/search. To search for your property, use either the address, the longitude/latitude coordinates, the county, a nearby road, or the state. This website will let you zoom in and move around to find your property. All of the flood zones are marked in blue or brown. If other properties that have sold recently also have flood zones, it's probably safe for yours to have one as well.

Marshland

When I heard about marshland, it made me think of swamps, marshes, and bogs, but it is so much more than that. Marshland is broadly classified as any land where water is close to the surface. You can't always tell if a property has marshland by looking at it. Like flood zones, marshland raises the price of insurance, but, unlike flood zones it is considered a protected area by the US government. You will probably NEVER get permission to build on marshland, not even with stilts. Marshland isn't necessarily a dealbreaker, but it does have the potential to decrease your resale value if it prohibits the buyer from building in every ideal spot. Proceed with caution!

You can look at a pretty good representation of marshland online at fws.gov/wetlands/data/Mapper.html. While not 100% accurate, it does give you a pretty good indication if you should be worried. (The only accurate marshland detection is to purchase a test from the local government). Click on the Wetlands mapper to look at your property. Even if you don't think that your property has a high chance of having marshland, you still need to do this check because marshland is literally everywhere.

Percolation Tests

Percolation is only important if your property does not have sewage. If the city has not expanded sewage to the area that you are investing in, it means that the buyer will have to install a septic tank. Septic systems are expensive but are installed when you build a house, so it isn't that big of a deal. However, what could be a big deal is if septic tanks won't work on your property. Percolation tests determine if they will!

Percolation is how quickly your soil allows water to

drain. Different areas on your property will perco-late at different speeds. One percolation test for one area could cost you as much as $150 to $1500! Here you might be thinking, "I have to check on this for every property?!". No. Absolutely not! A quick and dirty way to see if percolation is likely viable for your property is to check if any of the surrounding properties have houses. If they do, that's a good sign that the soil can percolate. You can do this by heading over to google earth, searching for the longitude of your property, and looking for roofs. I tell you how to do this in detail over in the next section - so stay tuned!

Most of the time, though, the worst-case scenario is the house can't be built where the buyers wanted it.

If you still feel a little nervous, I want to remind you that you will be purchasing these properties for pennies on the dollar. If your site is one of the unlucky .001% that fails the percolation test every-where, you can just lower the price and sell it to a buyer who doesn't need percolation. Very few investors end up getting burned by a lack of percola-tion. As always, you'll have to weigh your risk vs. reward tolerance.

That said, if you do need to order a percolation test,

the local county clerk's office can help. Give them a call and ask how much it will be and when they can get you on their schedule for a percolation test.

Visual Property Check

As a man of the cyber age, it always surprises me when you need to visually check anything... but your eyes are your best tools when investing in land. You need to check if your potential investment has junk on it AND if the neighboring properties look ok. The motivated seller probably lives out of state and likely hasn't seen his property for a while, so there's no guarantee that other random people haven't dumped anything.

There are two different ways to visually check for junk on and around your property - one is free and less accurate while the other is cheap and accurate.

The free way is using Google maps to look at your prospective property. Go on google earth and type in the address of your land (or if you don't have that, the latitude and longitude. Or, if you don't have that, you can type in a nearby street and search for it). Once there, you can get a bird's eye view. Zoom in and look around. Make sure you don't see anything strange.

If there are roads nearby, you can use Google Streetview to see the parts of your property that face the road. Place the Streetview man in front of your property. If you look in the top left corner of your screen, you should see a box. At the very bottom of that box, you should see the words "Street View". It isn't always available, but next to "Street View", you might see a clock. If you click on that, you can see when the most recent street view picture was taken and even go back in time. If the street view picture is less than six months old, then it is probably accurate. If it isn't, then you are rolling the dice.

If you want to be sure that the property looks good, you have two choices. You can hire someone on craigslist ($50) or use a professional service($150). Either way, they will go to the property, take pictures, and send them to you. They should also take pictures of the neighboring properties from the street so you can inspect them as well. If you can't find anyone on craigslist, or would prefer a profes-sional, I recommend https://wegolook.com/ products/standard-looks/vacant-land-inspection. The price depends on the property's location and size, but there's no harm in asking them how much it would be.

Sometimes, if you're working with a realtor, they can also go visually inspect the property for you. However, they will expect to be compensated as well.

If you're really broke, google maps and the word of your seller is your best bet - but if you have gone through all of the other due diligence steps and want to buy the property, getting pictures is definitely 10x better!

Gis Map

Remember when I said you need to make sure there is a gis map of your potential property online? Well, this is the time to check it. The FEMA flood zone website has property lines as well. You should make sure that the GIS property lines match up with the FEMA flood zone property lines. Go on Zillow. If there are property lines there, make sure they match up as well. Finally, when you get more of the official documents from your seller, make sure the property lines match up. If a discrepancy exists, you want to catch it early. But don't worry, if you happen to miss the discrepancy, your title company will probably catch it.

OTHER FEES

There are a few more costs associated with buying and selling land that you may forget about in all the excitement of performing due diligence. You need to figure in the "hidden" costs of purchasing land so you know you will for sure make a profit. The last thing I want is for you to be surprised. I briefly discussed these costs earlier in chapter 1 as closing costs and holding costs, but I want to break it down further here now that it's relevant.

Property Taxes, HOA fees, and Assessments Owed

Your due diligence should have found if the seller owes any back taxes, HOA fees, or assessments. If they do, you have to pay them before you can assume ownership. Sometimes, you can call the lien holders and make a deal, but to be safe, make sure you include the full amount owed in your calculations.

Purchase - Closing Costs

Usually, closing costs are covered by the seller, but since you are an investor, these closing costs will come out of your profit. Part of the reason people choose to work with investors is because they can "just get it over with". So I recommend that you include closing costs as part of your package.

If you purchased this land for more than a few hundred bucks, it's probably going to be worth it to close through a Title company(~$500). There are many benefits to closing through a title company. First, they check the title to make sure that there aren't any outstanding fees or discrepancies. They also make sure that the right people sign and all the money is correctly disbursed. I do list all the documents you need to close on your own later in the book though, so stay tuned if that's the way you want to go.

Photography

You do need a few pictures to sell a property. If you hired someone to take pictures as part of your due diligence, just use those. Photos aren't totally necessary because you can market your land with a picture from google maps and the parcel map (GIS map) we found earlier. But, if the market is saturated with other land deals, professional photos will set you apart.

If you determine you need photos, you have a few options. If you are close, you can take them yourself.

If you got pictures from the seller that are semi-recent, you can use those. Otherwise, you probably need to hire someone from Craigslist, Facebook Marketplace or Wegolook. Do not use fake pictures.

Sales Agent Commission

If you use a Real Estate Agent to sell the property, they will take around 10%. I do not recommend using an agent to sell land because there are tons of free places that work just as well. We will talk about each of these places in chapter 5.

As I've said before - land is a niche and most agents don't specialize in it so they won't know how to market it properly anyway.

Sale - Closing Costs

You also have to cover the closing costs for the sale. I would recommend using a title company here as well because you will probably be making thousands of dollars. Knowing everything was filed correctly is worth the money, trust me. In a few pages, I'll tell you about a double close which will cut your closing costs in half, but for now, add both the purchase closing costs and sales closing costs to your due diligence worksheet.

How Much Can I Sell For?

Now that you know everything about your potential investment, you need to know how much you can get for it.

So, how do we do that?

We check on the average price per acre!

You can use the average price per acre that you calculated earlier. However, now that you know which utilities are on your land, it might change which properties you use as comps. If the surrounding area is similar, you can use the price per acre you calculated earlier. However, if it is not, then calculate it again with land that has similar utilities, plant coverage, road access, +-10% of the acreage, HOA status, and flood zones (if applicable). Make sure you find at least three good comps in the area. Once you have the price per acre, multiply it by your acreage to find your average sales price.

To find out how much you will sell this property for, do the following equation.

.8 * Average Sales Price = Sales Price

. . .

To find out how much you want to purchase this property for, do the following equation

.1 * Average Sales Price = Minimum Purchase Price

.3 * Average Sales Price = Maximum Purchase Price

You might be wondering who would accept an offer as low as 10% of the perceived value of their land. The answer? About 1% of the people you market to. This 1% is the true motivated seller. They want to get rid of their land, and they want to do it NOW! They are usually just happy to receive some money for it instead of having to pay taxes each year.

This is just my rule of thumb - you could find that a different price is much better for your business! Maybe you start offering 50% of the purchase price. Do what fits your business. If you start getting a bunch of angry calls, you might consider raising the purchase price for that area. It all depends on what you are willing to accept as a profit margin vs how long you can wait to make a deal.

Some people believe that a deal with less of a profit is better than no deal at all. I tend to lean towards that camp, but only to the point that I'm still profitable. Don't let my rule of thumb get in the way of making your business successful. Different prices work for different people - part of the game is figuring out what yours is.

Should I buy?

Now that you have all the due diligence done, you can make an informed decision on whether or not to purchase the property. Investing is difficult because there are thousands of unique situations, and it's up to you to figure out if yours is a deal.

Try to think about the deal like you are the end buyer. Put yourself in their shoes. Since you're giving them such a great deal, they may be willing to overlook a *few* imperfections, but if your land is kinda crappy, no one will want to buy it. Make sure you know exactly how much you need to break even and what your desired profit margin is.

Use the below calculation to calculate profit:

Sales Price - Other Fees - Purchase Price = Profit

Keep in mind that a profit of a few hundred bucks is much riskier than a couple thousand because if something goes wrong, you run the risk of losing your entire profit and even some of your money.

Lots of new land investors are READY to buy land.

And since you're super ready to get your first deal, you're more likely to make mistakes. That's why I recommend you use landwatch/landhub for your first deal. Once you get your feet wet, you know what you're doing and your momentum will carry you forward. I know, I know, the landhub/landwatch deals are more expensive and I said you could do this with no money. Don't worry, I'm going to cover exactly what you need to do to find money in the next chapter.

Action Item: Make sure you have a spreadsheet with all of the due diligence calculations!

4

HOW TO BUY LAND, EVEN WHEN YOU'RE BROKE

There is nothing more satisfying than finding and buying your first deal... well, except for selling it! It's a testament to your hard work, and it's proof that you're doing all the right things. If you're at that point now, you're probably beyond excited and more than a little scared. That's natural for someone who hasn't closed their first deal. I'm sure you're wondering about what paperwork you need, you're scared your due diligence isn't quite right, and you probably haven't even thought through to the end to see how you're going to sell the damn thing! But don't worry, I am here to tell you what you need to do.

First and foremost, let's talk about money. If you have enough money saved up to buy this property outright, then great job! You can still read the next section because you might see a strategy you like more. After all, part of the draw of investing in real estate is to leverage our capital.

If you don't have all the money you need for the deal, stay tuned because I'm about to show you several ways to find it.

I'm Dead Broke

Fortunately for you, getting land under contract doesn't require a lot of money. To get a land deal under contract, you just draft up a purchase agreement and ask the seller to sign it. A purchase agreement is the legal document which asserts that you, the buyer, have sole rights to purchase this property. No one else can legally buy this property so long as you are within the terms of the purchase agreement. There are a few basic things you need in this contract

- Address of the land
- Full legal description of the land
- The purchase price
- The Earnest fee (If applicable in your state)
- The Escrow
- Grace period

• Closing date

A quick note here - make sure that you check your state laws because some states require the seller to pay an earnest fee to secure the contract. Luckily, this will only run you about $20. There is also this concept of a grace period in many states   a period of time in which the buyer can back out of the deal for any reason for no penalties. The grace period is not necessarily the entire term of the contract, but it can be if you write it that way. I do not intend to give you any legal documents because I am not a lawyer, but I advise you to use RocketLawyer.com. They will draft an air-tight contract that you can use over and over again.

Now that you have your deal safely under contract, how are you going to pay the seller?

Partnering

Partnering is exactly what it sounds like - you can either go to your local REI club or search the Facebook clubs for a partner. Make sure they are familiar with land investing (If you are going to your local club) before you tell them about your deal. As I mentioned earlier, you want to make sure you have a grace period for the entire term of the contract, so if a few of these investors say you have a bad deal, you can terminate it and move on. Of course, if the seller is willing to negotiate, try to find a win/win scenario before you terminate.

Some of these investors will say yes to partnering with you. Let them know that you have no money, but you are willing to enter into a 70/30 partner split as long as they finance the deal. They would get 70% because you want to make it enticing for them to put up their money. Even if you don't get all of the profit from the deal, you still did a deal and now have first-hand experience - which is worth its weight in gold! This is how you find a coach with 0$.

Loans

If you don't like the idea of partnering with someone, you can also take out a loan. Banks do not usually make loans on raw land, so you'll have to get a little creative. Luckily, many hard money lenders are more than happy to give you a loan. The best place to find hard money lenders is on the Land Investing Facebook groups because other investors will let you know if a particular company is any good. The downside of hard money lenders is the interest rate - it can be anywhere from 5%-10%. You also have to pay a few points on the deal.

If you don't want to take out a loan with a hard money lender, you have an LLC set up and you have good credit, you can apply for a business line of credit. A business line of credit is essentially a credit card for a business that acts like cash. For those financial professionals out there - please don't kill me for saying that!

Like a credit card, your business line of credit has a limit on how much you can spend and will not charge you anything if you don't have a balance. They are also very similar to a credit card because when you spend money, you are charged a percentage to borrow it. That said, business lines of credit differ from credit cards in a few key ways.

1. There is huge potential for a low interest rate - I've even seen some as low as 2%! (Though that is NOT typical. Normally it's somewhere between 4 and 7 if you have great credit.) If you opened an LLC, your interest rate depends largely on your personal credit score. Most big banks will look at your personal score and use that instead of any score your business has, especially if your business is new.

2. You can use it like cash. If you want to use it

to pay for land, you can withdraw from your
business line of credit as if it was a cash
account.

Double Close

If you don't like loans and can't find a partner, you
can try to do a double close - where you buy and sell
the land at the same time. Warning! Before you
attempt this strategy, google to see if it is legal in
your target investment state.

The title company will take care of the double close
and cut you a check for the remaining balance at the
end. Each close happens in different rooms so the
seller and end buyer do not know they are doing a
deal with anyone but you. This is necessary because
they each think the land is worth a different amount.
The seller will be selling you the land for a lower
price and the end buyer will be buying the land at a
higher price. You collect the difference as profit.

This is a powerful strategy, but it can be challenging
because you need to find a buyer before you close
with the seller. If you want to use this method, try to
push the close date out as far as the seller and the
state's laws will let you. If you find an end buyer
early - you can always ask the seller to sign a new

contract that pushes the date up. If you can't find a buyer in time, you have a few options: try to get an extension on your close date, find another way to pay for the deal, or terminate the contract.

Negotiating When You've Never Negotiated Before

Some sellers will answer your marketing material because they are curious. Others will be in a dire situation and need the money. Some may be tired of paying taxes on land they never visit or use. There are a million reasons to sell land and it's up to you to determine which reason your seller has.

As I mentioned before, you want to be nice and respectful to motivated sellers. People want to do deals with people they like. If they don't like you, then they are less likely to follow through on the deal. You want to be pleasant and chatty so you can use the opportunity to find out more about them. For instance, why are they selling the land? Sure, you need to know if there is anything wrong with the land, but you also want to understand the seller's motivation and pain. Once you figure that out, you should tailor your conversation to revolve around that point.

For instance, if they are tired of spending money on land they never use or see, you should talk about what they would rather do with the money they spend on their land each year. Make them start daydreaming.

On the flip side, if they need help because they are late on their taxes or are about to have their land foreclosed on, you should address their fears. Let them know you'll handle it all for them. Stress that you will take care of it, and they won't have to worry about it anymore. What are they worrying about anyway? *You're going to pay them to save their credit.*

Make sure they understand that you are purchasing the land as is. What that means for the seller is they don't need to deal with realtors, and they don't need to fix up their property. You can also offer to close on their schedule. If they want to close in a week, then try to make that happen. If they want to hang onto the land for a few more months, no problem! Just include it in the purchase agreement.

Once you've learned why they want to sell the land, you can use that to negotiate. You absolutely will buy it for less than they could sell it for if they sold it using the MLS. Do not tell them you are buying it for a low rate. They likely already know they aren't getting as much out of their land as they could - but most of them understand that you are giving them a quick and easy sale. If they complain, you should remind them about not using a realtor and as-is condition. If they continue to complain, tell them something like, "Well, I know land in the area is taking half a year to sell, but you might get a higher price if you use a realtor. You'll probably have to pay 10% of what you get for selling, clean all the junk off your land and get professional photos taken, but I think you could squeeze out a little more if you're willing to do the work." then, give them the name and number of the realtor you've been working with. Make sure you call back in a few weeks to check on their progress. Do not offer to buy the land from them if they are using a realtor because you will have to pay the realtor fees, and it is seldom worth your time.

Remember, do not go above the 30% mark. Not everyone who calls you will be someone who sells you land. You don't want to have all of your money caught up in a bad deal when a great one finally shows up. Trust me, great ones will come as long as you stick to the process! That's not to say you can't negotiate, just make sure you start low enough to leave room.

Closing Your Deal

Closing a real estate deal is different in every state. Some states require that you use a title company or lawyer. Other states don't have that requirement. Every state has different paperwork that you have to fill out, and each state has a different process. If you are trying to close a very tiny deal that only nets you $1000 in profit, it might be worth your time to close on your own. Self-close involves doing some paperwork and paying a notary around $200 to file it for you.

You can find a traveling notary in the area you are investing in by searching "Mobile Notary <county>". The notary will be able to take you through the exact process that you need to follow and might be able to direct you to the necessary closing documents. They will probably not be able to answer your questions on how to close it - figuring that out is up to you. If you really want to save a couple hundred bucks and don't mind doing paperwork, then go for it!

If you choose to use a title company, they do all of the legwork for you. Title companies make sure that the right people sign, that there are no unexpected liens on the property, that there are no problems with the deed/title, and that the money is disbursed correctly. You can find title companies by doing a google search "Title company <county>". It is much easier to use a title company than close on your own, so if you find that you are short on time or you don't want to do the research necessary to fill out the closing documents, then a title company is the way to go.

If you still want to close on your own, you will need the following documents (at a minimum!). You can find examples online, but I suggest you have an attorney draft them up if you choose not to use a title company.

- Your signed purchase agreement
- A Land Contract
- A Memorandum of Land Contract
- The Deed
- Closing Statement

Action Item: Make sure you have all the documents you need to close the deal! Make sure you've researched double close laws in the state you are investing in! Make sure you find a great local Title company! It's worth it to call the title company even before you need them to figure out their pricing structure and workflow.

5

STRATEGIES FOR MAKING INSANE ROI IMMEDIATELY

This is the final step before you can cash your check! All you have to do is post your deal and wait for the sellers to come to you! In this chapter, we are going to talk about where to post your deal, how to market your property, and the strategies you use to turn your dirt into cash.

SELLING

I am not going to pretend that this book covers every single selling strategy that land investors use, but I will touch on the more popular ones.

Selling Outright

The first strategy is to sell the land outright. The benefit is obvious - you get all the money right then! Congrats! You can turn around and invest it in the next few deals. This is a great strategy for building capital, but if you're trying to quit your day job, it's not the one to use long term. This strategy is far from passive because to make money, you must find more deals. However, it's great when you are getting started because it quickly generates more money for more deals.

Seller Financing

Many investors prefer to steer their prospective buyers towards seller financing rather than purchasing the property outright. Seller financing is when you take a down payment and finance out the rest. That's right, seller financing is when you become the bank! For instance, you could ask for a 10% down payment and charge them 7% interest for 3 years! You might be wondering why anyone would agree to those terms, especially in today's market, where interest rates are dirt cheap (3% average for our future readers). As I mentioned earlier, banks do not mortgage raw land, so your buyer will have a hard time finding a bank that would be willing to give them a loan. AND, if they do find a bank, they will probably have to put 20% or more down. Lots of Americans want to be landowners, but they don't have the money for a 20% down payment, let alone the entire purchase price of the land! That's where you come in.

You can attract people like this by putting Seller Financing in your ad. I will show you an example further down that is almost guaranteed to attract someone who wants to take advantage of your crazy seller finance deal. You can reuse the same legal paperwork as before, except it would give the buyer all the benefit (They could leave at any time!). You should either try to edit the document yourself, ask your lawyer to make the document so you can change the earnest fee (to 1% when you are selling and $20 when you are buying) and the grace period (to 3 days when you are selling and the term when you are buying), or have 2 separate purchase agreements filled out.

All of the other documents I talked about earlier will also be necessary to close and should have similar edits made. If you choose to use RocketLawyer, make sure you mention these stipulations when you get your contract made.

Seller Financing is the best way to turn land into

passive income. Each property might only be a term of 2-5 years, but at least you have guaranteed income for that time. That means if you want to take a vacation for a few months, you don't have to worry. An even bigger bonus: you aren't renting, so the buyer will not call you if there are problems.

Some of you may be wondering what would happen if the buyer stops paying you. It's simple - you fore-close. I won't say it never happens because you might be dealing with people who have pretty low credit, but it doesn't happen often. When it does, you'll probably be out a few months of their payment until the foreclosure goes through. But once you get through that, you can just sell your land again.

Another benefit to seller financing is interest. Interest absolutely skyrockets your returns - how do you think credit card companies stay in business? Shameless plug alert! If you are interested in investing in debt, I have another book coming out that you can read called Stacked. You can go to www.beauxblast.com/notes for more information.

Subdividing

Another strategy is to subdivide your land. There are entire books based on this topic so I thought it was worth a mention. It can be very profitable because splitting one huge lot into many smaller lots means that you can collect more down payments, more monthly mortgage payments, and more interest.

The first step is to look at your due diligence sheet to see what your land's legal description is. Next, you need to call the county courthouse to see if there are any zoning or subdivision regulations. You might have to explain what you are trying to do to them and will probably get transferred a few times, but you will eventually find someone who can help you. Sometimes, rural areas don't have any regulations, and the process is as simple as filing some paperwork.

If the zoning regulations allow you to subdivide your land, you can move on to the next step - checking the subdivision regulations. Subdivision regulations hold the legal requirements to subdivide your land. Once you know what legal requirements you should follow, you can draw out a plat which is a map of your subdivision. A surveyor or engineer often draws these.

Use Zillow to determine if there is a market for the size of plots that you want to sell. Sometimes, when you're way out in the country, people don't want tiny land plots. They'll want at least an acre. Why else would they move all the way out there?!

Once you've determined there is a market, you should use Zillow to determine the price of each of those lots by doing the same exercise we did during your due diligence. You need to do this again because small lots and big lots may have a different price per acre. I know it's frustrating to do the same thing over and over again, but now that you've read the book all the way through, you'll know what to do next time. If I gave you all of this information at once, it would be extremely confusing.

The local planning staff and a planning commission will review your plat, which will then be approved and recorded by the local courthouse. Once that is done, you can sell your subdivided land!

I recommend you only try to subdivide if your property has a road running along one of its long edges because then you don't need to build roads and utilities will be relatively cheap to install. Trust me, subdivision gets very complicated and expensive once you start building roads!

RENTING

The last major strategy is to rent out the land. One strategy is to find farmers, hunters, or ranchers in the area who want to rent your land. It's not very lucrative, but it will probably pay your yearly taxes. If you have confidence that this land will be worth a lot one day because the town is expanding, this is probably worth it. If you choose to rent to farmers, you might also be eligible for exemptions that will decrease your taxes!

You could also improve the land and then rent what you improved. There are many different strategies: You could buy tiny homes, mobile homes, or trailers and rent those out. You can build houses and rent those out. You could build a hunting lodge and rent that out. There are hundreds of strategies you can use if you want to own land and rent it out - use your imagination!

For instance, tiny homes. You will have to check with your state's laws, but normally if you have a nonpermanent structure that is under 400 square feet, it is treated as personal property. Personal property is taxed way less than a proper building, at least in my investment state - Texas! You also might be able to get away with not subdividing the land.

That means you can put a bunch of tiny homes on your property and rent them out to Airbnbers or people interested in living a sustainable life. If your land does not have utilities going to it, you can still pursue this strategy, but you'll have to get creative! There are off the grid tiny homes that you can buy, but they are a little pricey. I would buy one used. Make sure it has solar panels, a rain catch, and a composting toilet - that way, you don't need electricity or running water!

You could also just rent out plots of land instead of the entire tiny home. However, you should proceed with this business strategy with caution because it might not work in every market.

If you don't like the idea of a tiny home, you could also put mobile homes on your land and rent those out. I know some investors who have found a lot of success with this technique. Check with that county's laws before you try this strategy. It can get pretty expensive, and it's not very beginner-friendly. Mobile homes do not have the same tax advantages as tiny homes and also usually require subdivision.

Renting is a great way to make income, but it is only semi-passive at best. You will be a lot more hands-on with your investments. Since it is still your property, you are expected to fix anything that goes wrong - If a toilet overflows at 4 am, guess whose phone rings. And if your renters decide to destroy your property, then you are responsible for fixing it. Renters are also more likely to stop paying you, and the eviction process is often long and drawn out. You could pay a property manager to take care of most of these problems for you - but keep in mind that it will eat into your profits. One of my next steps is to own a mobile home park - and I will definitely be hiring staff to take care of the park. However, these expenses add up fast so you must make sure you are profitable before you pursue it!

Don't get me wrong, lots of investors make a lot of money renting - after all, you own that property forever! But it isn't all rainbows and sunshine either.

Where Do I Sell?

You might think the only place to sell your land is on the MLS. This isn't true at all! Most land investors find that they have an easier (and cheaper!) time selling their deals on free sites. Zillow.com,

Craigslist.com, landhub/landwatch and redfin are great examples of free or small fee-based sites! I'll skip through the step by step how-to for posting FSBO on those sites I mentioned because it's fairly straightforward.

Remember those pictures we talked about earlier? Make sure you remember to put them in your ads! People love to fantasize, so you need to give them something to fantasize about. Make sure the very first photo that people see on your listing is the most beautiful of the bunch. Focus on water features, wide-open plains, or even a beautiful treed area. Make sure you put a picture that will catch their eye!

As for the ad copy, include the following:

- The size
- This property is marketed to sell and won't last long
- A message about their dreamhouse (If applicable)
- Highlights of any of the beautiful features from the pictures above
- Seller financing available
- You could be a landowner for this ridiculously small down payment!

- Utilities (If applicable)

For example:

10 Acres available!
I have 10 acres available with utilities in a great part of town! There is a beautiful pond on the property that would be a wonderful view from your dream home. It's priced to sell so call now because this deal won't last long! SELLER FINANCING AVAILABLE! If you've got $250 for a downpayment, you could be a landowner TODAY. Call for more details 555-555-5555!

I also want to mention - if you did end up purchasing a seller's site you should post your deals here as well. The seller site will need to be marketed somehow so you will either have to have it optimized or advertised. You can advertise it for free by posting on Facebook marketplace in the beginning and then slowly ramp up to advertising your website later on.

Another strategy is to purchase a sign for your land and advertise seller financing. You can purchase a sign from a local print shop and hire someone from Craigslist, Facebook marketplace, or even the print shop to put it up for you! Local people will drive by every day. The more exposure your ads get, the more likely someone is to purchase it. This advertising method is not free, so it might not be your preferred method if you're just starting out.

Action Item: Get some eyes on your deal by putting it up on those websites or using a sign.

6

BONUS CHAPTER!

I'm about to wrap this book up, but I wanted to say a few things before I did. First, I highly recommend you find your first deal from a wholesaling land website. It's not going to be as profitable, but what you will learn from the semi-safe environment of dealing with other investors will definitely give you the confidence to talk to tentative sellers.

Once you do your due diligence and find a great deal on landhub or landwatch, you need to pick your favorite way of paying for it and then start advertising seller financing. Even if you sell it for the exact same amount you bought it for(Try not to!), you will still gain 3 very important things.

1. You will still make money because of interest. If you charge a 5% interest, the rule of 72 says it would only take 15 years to double your money. (If you divide 72 by your interest rate, it will give you approximately the number of years it takes to double your money at that interest rate.) While you probably wouldn't owner finance them for 15 years (more like 3 or 5) it gives you a good understanding that you will make some money from the interest. I give a whole rundown of how this works in my note investing book. www.beauxblast.com/notes if you're interested in learning more.

2. You will gain experience. That's right, each new deal gives you more experience. Who would have thought?

3. You will gain confidence. The more confidence you gain, the easier it will be to do the next deal.

So there you have it, your first goal is to start perusing landhub and landwatch, doing your due diligence, and making offers.

One you've completed a few deals from there, you

can start to implement the marketing techniques I recommended earlier.

I hope that makes sense.

Happy hunting!

CONCLUSION

If you enjoyed this book, it would mean a lot to me if you left a 5-star review and a comment about one thing you learned. I tried to write a book that I would have LOVED as a beginner, how did I do? If you want to communicate with me directly, join my list by going to land.beauxblast.com.

I hope that you were following along and now have a deal! If not, I am confident that you have everything you need to get started. Success loves speed, so buying a book with beginner-friendly information and action items is a cheap way to hit the ground running.

You can find the action items as well as all of the

resources I've mentioned on my website - www.BeauxBlast.com/Land. I really hope this book gives you the push you need to get started!

Thanks for reading! I'll see you out there...

Beaux Blast

LAND INVESTING CHECKLIST BUNDLE

(SUPERCHARGE YOUR BUSINESS!)

THIS COMPANION BUNDLE INCLUDES:

- A Quickstart checklist for finding your perfect investment area
- The Due Diligence Checklist: NEVER miss a due diligence step again
- A BONUS FLOWCHART: Busting through common seller objections

The last thing we want is for you to start investing in unprofitable land and give up. Download this bundle to STOP that from happening.

To receive your Land Investing Checklist Bundle, visit the link:

LAND.BEAUXBLAST.COM

CPSIA information can be obtained
at www.ICGtesting.com
Printed in the USA
BVHW030203010822
643474BV00022B/575